THE TRADITION

PRINCETON SERIES OF CONTEMPORARY POETS

For Other Books in the Series, see p. 136

A. F. MORITZ

THE TRADITION

Princeton University Press

Published by
Princeton University Press,
41 William Street,
Princeton, New Jersey 08540

In the United Kingdom:
Princeton University Press,
Guildford, Surrey

Library of Congress Cataloging in
Publication Data will be found on
the last printed page of this book

ISBN 0-691-06667-1 (cloth)
      0-691-01427-2 (pbk)

Publication of this book has been
aided by a grant from the Paul
Mellon Fund of Princeton Univer-
sity Press

This book has been composed
in Linotron Optima

Clothbound editions of Princeton
University Press books are printed
on acid-free paper, and binding
materials are chosen for strength
and durability. Paperbacks, al-
though satisfactory for personal
collections, are not usually suita-
ble for library rebinding

Printed in the
United States of America
by Princeton University Press
Princeton, New Jersey

To my mother

and to the memory of my father

CONTENTS

ACKNOWLEDGMENTS

Some of these poems have appeared in the following magazines: *The Connecticut River Review, The Dalhousie Review, Descant* (Texas Christian University), *Descant* (Toronto, Canada), *The Fiddlehead, Four by Four, The Greenfield Review, The Malahat Review, The Memphis State Review, Nebula, Poetry Canada Review, Quarry, The Tamarack Review, Webster Review,* and *West Coast Review.* "Putting Up for the Night," "Dwarf World," "Reflection," and "The Difference" first appeared in a pamphlet, *Putting Up for the Night,* published by Northern Lights Publishers, London, England; "The Helmsman Palinurus" first appeared in *Mirages,* the catalogue of an exhibition by Ludwig Zeller and Susana Wald, published by Galérie Surréaliste, Toronto, Canada. Grateful acknowledgment is also made to the Ingram-Merrill Foundation and the Canada Council for grants supporting the writing of this book.

PART I

THE TRADITION

- I think we are the inheritors of slaves,
  a race of water bearers to the patient herd.

But whose memory reaches so far back?
We can see how quickly the children of our day
forget the names of their parents newly dead.
No documents are found in our houses.
No object we make will last two generations.
No skills are handed down
but how to live each day with the flies, the wind
that veers and whips the dust ever replenished,
and distant shouting, random sirens at night.

In these sheds between compulsive howl and silence,
between young and old, what knowledge falls?
Now and again some few among our proverbs
are shown by science to be not wholly meaningless.
Our habits bear resemblance to religion,
our jokes to story. Scholars discuss our culture,
whether vestigial or primitive;
whether by instinct or tradition we patch
hovels of newspaper, boxes, corroded tin
in barren lots sown with splinters of bricks;
whether there is some reason in our claim
that a calm word from this or that deathbed
has exalted starvation, typhus, and mute lethargy.
Our only leisure, afforded by long moments

straining with constricted bowels, gives rise
to pride in our own penetration,
our contempt of self-denial, our ignorance of pleasure.

More than any future,
we want the past to have been marvelous.
Ancestors: these are our one invention.
Pirates, smugglers, revolutionaries.
Beachcombers piling shells, staring over the sea.
Magi of forgotten disciplines,
the content of their researches beyond us—
although the banal formulas that survive
are full of implication.

And the real fathers?
Those who in fact dropped sperm in broken cisterns,
moaning to create us? There is no way to know them,
unless to presume that they were much like us.
Then, at times, they too
felt themselves cherishers of the fire that hides,
inscribes itself only in ash, and like some toad
endures centuries in a toppled well,
sleeping under the rim stones with their forgotten script.
On clear nights in the lanes of the warehouse district,
they too must have glimpsed the setting moon—
its blurred figures buried in watery light—
and claimed it theirs, as the only beings
still conscious in that place and at that hour.

CHILDHOOD OF A SCIENTIST

- Long past the age for speaking
  still silent, not wanting anything,
  I did not understand I had been born
  to parents deaf and mute.

  All day in the shaded rooms
  for rhythm the clock,
  for melody the stirring of a mouse,
  for harmony the whirr and tap
  of insects baffled by glass.

  All day in a town of clapboard and dust,
  a grid imprinted on a burnt-up sea,
  all day wandering among remnants of that sea.
  A collection of stones and polished claws.
  Silence of grasses, hunting birds
  and the hunting sun shadowing victims
  pricked with its arrow,
  infused with its slow poison.
  I watched it follow patiently
  all day,
  waiting for them to drop.

  On a shelf of bank thrust out
  into the river, shaded and screened by cottonwoods,
  alone I built, I launched
  and with a barrage of stones
  I sank my brittle fleets.

By wagon one day, clownish tragedians came.
From a hard pew in the bare wooden hall
I heard lame Richard rave
for a kingdom nowhere to be seen:
words that rolled and soaked and pelted more
than rain with hail and thunder
down in the crops while people wait in fear.

The kingdom of the tiger lily
was passing that month in watery hollows.
On the road at night going home
I found a papery wing and kept it,
and silence returned
as I walked under the late summer stars.

THE EXPLORER

- Here among the forks and plates
  they want me to remember and describe.

  I remember this much:
  there weren't any words in the white deserts, skies, and tombs,
  no words in the north,
  only green empty air, black limbs, low grey rock
  by planes of steely water, and ice in shadows.

  Since I came back, all of the words I know
  have been wandering in me among those remembered things.
  Never yet has one word found a place,
  not even a tree or a profile in a cliff
  to stop at, to remind it of why it came.

  Despite the winds that blow there,
  I can still hear the questions.
  To appease these talkers I would almost tell them
  how quiet I am in those places.
  I wander there, small and alone,
  and everything seems familiar, a part or power of myself,
  yet nothing recognizes me.
  And if I stayed, nothing would save my life.

  Even now, while my hand lies with stainless steel and glass,
  my feet are in the sand or snow,
  huge cliffs or flats around me, always the huge sky,
  and they are in me as I'm in them.

But I can't reach or touch them.
I never can enter them deeply enough
or take them far enough down into me.
So much love, such hunger: I've brought back nothing else
and this failure, wonder, silence is my life.

THE BONE HUNTER

Red Deer River badlands, Alberta, Canada

- If from the fiery rock on which I stand
a claw could rise, I would welcome it.
The heat, the clear air, the blazing sky, to me
are mere barrier to the world I seek.
And the striation of the cliffs: a stair
of colors, a prism leading down
into eighty million years ago—but always
to ruin, silence, this empty mineral jaw
where my hammer clanks, dwarfed in the silence of sun.
O let me not be trapped and memorized
in this stone of brightness, like a word, but let
the dreary wind rise now in the sparse cottonwoods
and a little motion, a little flashing of leaves
transport me. What place would be mine in that world
I strive to see? To have no knowledge but sail
the inland ocean down birdless coasts,
insect-ridden, along the cypress swamps,
the reptiles' dominion of sleep
without effort or error enveloping
a world of so much time, more time,
more peace than I can guess . . .
Those drowned shores, where every life
is compounded of what it is with something else,
that which it was or is to be:
the snake drags withered feet, a fish
gasps in the air, the mammals
dive deep to lay their eggs—all watched
by crabs perched high on the tree bark.

All prophesy without knowledge.
And there would I remain this thing
that gives voice, causing what it foretells?
But let me sail once where all is undiscovered,
perhaps forgetting even speech and desire,
a loving eye in the festival of carbon.

ARCHAEOLOGIST OBSERVING
AN EXCAVATION

- Once again we come to unearthed reflections,
fragments perhaps of knowing's deepest floor:
blinding, and always throwing the blank shape
of their old light over all. They blaze:
human figures and tablets of burnt clay
cut free from earth as the diggers work,
approaching the virgin clay beneath
the last level of ancient settlement.

And the diggers—they too are fragments of old clay.
Or beings from before the clay, from years
when clay's elements drove through the air,
grains of water and sand, desire
that never yet had imagined any union.
And there were no witnesses, unless these diggers
were present in the first mating of things—
if mating, desire, are words that touch creation.

Flakes of light on grass and water,
birds in wild apple trees, the doubled bodies
scratching earth, baring ancient reflections—
words pass among them all,
brushing the dirt away, seizing on some,
setting them in the silent sphere of the eye:
loved ghosts are seen once more on earth,
then earth rises, and they are buried again:

untouched, unknown, leaving the same desire.
And so once more we come to echoes that rebound
among reflections. Syllables swim in lights,
dazzling glints off bold things,
images canonized by fame,
the reflex of a face on water dark or bright,
on time flowing over the planet, on the sky
abstract with stars or cut open by the sun.

THE PAINTER

- Is life wasted staring over the sea?
This is the way I worship the beachcomber god,
lord of driftwood that has wandered for years
to stop now at my feet. I stare,
for what is there to see? At night
only twelve animals that foolishness
places among the stars. This life
wants no place in their wheel: it flashes
once from the earth, a fish leaping,
and vanishes. By day I see shacks and trees,
the burning paleness between ocean and sky,
thin, almost absent shades of violet,
one part murex in a million parts of brine:
sustaining light, the painter's element,
pastel, pale to the point of nonexistence.

Stare at the sea, choke
in the dusty power the sun has over it.
Liquid desert. Theater of hallucination.
Whoever goes there will see what may be seen:
men with the heads of birds, men with noses
that are long spatulas for taking bread from the oven,
men with one eye, one ear, one arm,
one buttock, one testicle: they hop over the waves.
Look. But let the desert saints
go first, encounter, clear away
all things that laugh at travelers through the waste,
the blank of water, life's source.

They say the devil comes there
in the form of a beautiful woman
to tempt men from their vows. I too desire
love, which is not proper to this life.
Here naked women—not anything in woman's form,
but women—pass on the beach all day. For most
I am too sick, but sometimes one will take me,
and such . . . they love my room
filled up with canvases,
the sound of my warped guitar, the slosh of gin.
This is what I am. They love
some aggregate of ocean sunsets,
the mood of pleasure pitted against time,
of idleness and resolute decay.
Nothing, sentiment, a minor chord
as crabs skitter in the crimson sheen
of wet sand at evening and morning.

Day by day this path up and down my beach,
this daubing at starfish, sandshrubs, driftwood
and all the wreckage of intimate disaster
washed here from the hotels or overseas.
A high-heeled shoe, a spar, a nylon, tangle together
in webs of kelp. The paint on the canvas
sags, boneless, tending to shades of weed
and oily sand. Only the blue
that needs no form is brilliant, clear,
and sends its splendor down lanes through the leaning shacks
and in the rotting forest. The moment captured here
sufficed, suffices, for itself, but not for me.
And I reject labor too, and am rejected.

This loud rhythm of silence, baffling glare,
this gaze of the horizon that sees all.
Is life wasted staring over the sea?

I have been here, my feet planted in sand
among the trees dropping limp chains of white flowers,
flashes off lacquered leaves, the twinkling destruction
of green in pure light . . . I have been here . . .
Is it spring? So many seeds are drifting,
it must be spring. But I have been here
all of a summer that never had a beginning.
Or it began, and ended, and I forget,
confused by the drooping ropes of petals
like strings of fishes caught and hung in the air.

A MAN OF POOR ORIGINS

- With great suffering, great sorrow, great expense
  my people sent me here, to this white tower
  set in a garden on the sea's opposite shore.
  And how can I return, what would I bring?
  Never have I reached the core of anything
  but only heard noise, remained in surfaces,
  the splendor and stink of surfaces. Nonetheless,
  I know myself: driftwood, a branch or spar
  cast up on the white sand under my window,
  the endless strand of cleanness along the ocean,
  eternally burnt and washed, haunted by crabs
  at twilight. Driftwood shows me what I am:
  a vegetable torso decaying in a blank
  perspective, sun-sterilized—a thing that rots
  without odor, not growing earthy and compost-soft
  but turning blond with pale white streaks, forgetting
  bark and birdlime and swarming ants, becoming
  dry and permanent.

                    Where now is the black
  clamor of life, even if a living string
  still binds it to the mud? In the villages
  thrown down on earth without foundation or root,
  the shacks slide in the rain, the children shift,
  the parents erode under the downpour's misery,
  torrents that pass unhindered through their roofs.
  My country, where water doesn't cleanse or lighten,
  but dissolves excrement in the alleys, floats

fruit rinds and spit-out seeds like little corpses
on a flood, and mixes all in such a paste
as no traveler can easily shake from his feet.
All night the rains would walk the road outside,
a shapeless animal, passing and passing.
We heard the featureless, soothing, boring rush
of water falling—falling like souls of the dead,
minds made blank by death and a thousand years
bathed in warm dews, but now thrown down to be born
on earth again for the sin of joyful pride
they committed in that other world: a pride
of rising up and shining, light and pure,
of floating toward the sun and merging in air
with dust to build the clouds, white liquid worlds
mimicking, in their suppleness surpassing
all that exists below.

                So, in the nights,
they were thrown down to the earth, and listening
we feared to go out even to relieve ourselves,
lying with swollen bladders, hearing the frigid
water dance on the tin roof and drip through.
What torment at last to flee into the road,
to finger the penis, to feel the small warm piddle,
its tiny noise, engulfed and destroyed in the flood,
and to come back, shivering, the rain still falling
from our hair onto our backs, between our buttocks,
and pierced with the fresh smells of earth and water
to sleep again until the fecal dawn.
Then heat would resurrect the odors—wraiths
that stood by every shed, at every corner,
each odor linked to a place, a guardian spirit.
And we'd see time passing in the hardening mud,
the refuse struggling there like swimmers: garbage
and the dog's corpse thrown out last week by now

swallowed from sight, and yesterday's tin cans
already half submerged.

                              "Because of you,"
so said the sun, "water will never again
thoroughly cleanse this earth." My people may be
the cities to be drowned, cities from which
the lash of the storm always draws back, restrained . . .
But they are also the ark built in day's dust
that rocks at night in the squalls, that almost floats,
and always morning finds it struck in the mud,
waiting again, as dead wood waits, amid
the laughter of wives and butchers who last night cried.
It never moves, but sometimes a twisted log
breaks off, floats to a distant beach, and someone
collects it, an emblem of rank life, though now
long dead, made white and suitable by time.

LAMENT OF A HUNTER

▪ In the halls and escalators of this castle
and sealed in its dungeons: the dessicating
sunlight that never clouds. The open-concept
spaces that curl on a green plain down
to watering places, lakes captured in crystal bulbs . . .
A mailed and greaved and mounted man,
or a naked runner with a spear, I course
the boundaries of the desk-top farms and curse
chicken wire, domestic swine, sheep filling narrow tracks.

Faith is this wandering in the parks that kindness
has set aside as if I were trailing the caribou
as when twice each year they used to cross our barrens. Sorrow
is these women who may praise magnificence
rarely, talking in their sound sleep, but take
not one who passes in a day or a week,
with the game or the wars, but the man who dies
as they do, imperceptibly, through years.

Violins have driven the monkeys' mockery and flight
from the forest of white, straight, branchless trunks.
Perpetually in training for nothing under the sun,
my chest swells and gleams as Hector's never did.
With the tattoo needle I draw caste and blood.
By night through clothes I have carefully clawed to a shred,
my nipples point like darts. And for a shield
in the back alleys I bang the trashcan lid.

PART II

THE LIST

- It occurred to me that we should write down the names of the dead.

Then it was necessary to have a system of measuring time
to write them down accurately, in order:
which one came first and which ones afterward.

At once, when that was done, I saw what poor memories we have,
and that everything we know is only poor memory.
People would talk to me of such-and-such a dead man
as of a great chief or evil spirit from the days of the giants.
But I had my list. I knew, and it was always thus:
the man they spoke of was a trembler and woman-beater
who had died in his sleep six or seven years ago.

Some day my list will be so long
that its keeper, when I am dead, will not know anything
about the men who had the names at the beginning.
Trying to know them from what I write,
he will know that he makes them up out of himself.

The list is now the dead. Never again will they
come back to triumph over me
in the fire and the darkness outside the fire.
I've done it. I've finally killed them. I've killed the dead.

THE DIFFERENCE

- Something there is that is no longer here.
  But the memory of what it is
  that is not here is taken away.
  And sometimes it seems that what is here
  cannot be real, for what it was is gone
  and the difference, lying between now and then,
  sucks all attention to itself.

  That the last year and this are different
  is what one knows. This leaf now held in a hand
  will escape entirely, and who can swear
  that one did not hold it like this,
  this one and not another, in other years
  before or still to come? But that can't be:
  the difference is known. Only the things
  that differ escape the mind, which howls on,
  wrapped in black, over its forgotten dead—
  so busy with grief that it forgets to die
  these thousand years wandering in its world-wide
  sarcophagus of flint and night air.

NOON, AUGUST FIELDS

- Because your body is memory
  of things you've never known and don't recall
  except in the body,
  look up. This summer the fields spread out
  through many years. Corn will come back first,
  then wheat, and the odor in the sway-backed barn,
  scent of wood dead of a dead axe.

In noon's stillness the crops ripple
with an inner breath
and shelter inner darkness as of a body:
a vast desire, tassled and rooted, moved and calm.
Each plant is forced to its use
and at last you will know it:
in the mouth and beneath the ribs,
brightness erect.

Now no one is in the fields.
Not the dead who plotted them long ago
and left here and there an isolated tree.
Not the living who hide themselves from this heat
in their white house, their work already legend:
this harvest on its way.

No one is in the fields.
But say that they are here, living and dead,
they are resting from their work. Then look up:
they lean on their elbows in the shade
and their children come out from the house, bringing them food.

TO SET LOVE IN ORDER

- Not childlike, not holy,
  not having attained what was meant in the beginning,
  we, when we died,
  spread no perfume of hastening presence through the air,
  our memory is not the oil
  on the breasts fullest of milk and pleasure,
  always at the lips of all.

  Still loved for our blood,
  still hated for every failure, we
  remain to trouble the living.

  Slowly our image fades to join
  the one
  question:
  has anything lived except to spoil?
  Dying, we added ourselves
  to this, the single abstract ghost
  all the too human dead must share.

  Beloved friends, you too,
  pressing your bodies in places where we were,
  now delay to set your love in order.

  Forgive us, you in whom
  our having lived dissolves to thicken
  the certainty that all is at an end.

ALIVE IN THE DAWN

- We are alive, they shouted, in the dawn . . .
the dawn of magic, science, wealth, and power.
Bitterly I used to regret it wasn't noon yet,
for I was a child no longer. Born too soon,
I'd die before I could see all men become
healthy and undeluded. I'd never study
the final explication of the cosmos.
I wouldn't live long enough to take the serum
of immortality—or they'd discover it
only in my old age, and I'd be left
with the temptation, the doubt, whether to make
my wrinkles and pain eternal. But this dawn,
it finally occurred to me, has been frozen here
since first I heard it announced some years ago,
since first it was announced in the old books and papers—
and it never climbs from its purples and blood reds
to any simple light. A needed dawn, perhaps,
always painted again over the sky.
So all is started and never finished but always
started again, and up ahead—where something
seems to be shining through this somber twilight
called dawn, though it looks as much like winter dusk—
is there safety? Will we reach it before we die?
And can we now, finally, cut ourselves from the ones
who won't be seen again, in any possible day
coming to us on earth?—O mother, father,
in the pre-dawn, rusted anchors in your wet graves.

DEAF PRESENCE

- O sun, O mother twilight gaining the green hills,
  I feel myself again
  meet you and lose again
  a faith that contradicts the earth,
  losing long grief for the dead
  and continual forgiveness that the dead alone
  can, if they hear us, give.

  Again it grows brief, the sorrow for the lost,
  and like a shadow in late afternoon
  thrown from a bald horizon, long—
  their deaf presence, invincible accusation
  in blank weather, in stones that chance to fall.

  And the sky is closing,
  the night sky grows over us again
  as hard and narrow as day,
  all fresh and dark repose, all widest brilliance
  are again the waiting places
  of a jaw, a holy fear;

  but the wound and its memory are closing too.
  A dance leads from the scar.
  Men and women end but the flesh is born.
  And again violent in me
  you claim the rite
  of deep indifference.

HAMMER STROKES

From the bourgeois piano as I play
no music comes, we hear only
the strokes of the hammers
building or breaking down a city.
I obey the ancient score. My skill
directs my hands, but what are these dull sounds?

A casement gleams, reflected in
the mahogany of the piano lid,
and your image stands beside it, looking out.
You see a river wind from the horizon.
It twists through an ice-like etching
of motionless autumn woods,
reaches at last the crumbling brick
warehouses, the huge black hangars of the mills.

Bearing curved bridges and white sails
and clusters of October wildflowers,
it finds its way to our place here.
It flows past the wall and trembles
in the strings, in the blood,
as we dress for evening's pain and gaiety.

Love, let me hold the door.
Let me start the careless car.
Let's leave the house tonight, leave it to them
who built it long ago and died

on the banks of this hallucination.
Forget your dream that they will tear it down
while we are gone. It won't happen tonight.
Nothing will happen for a long time yet.

CIRCUS FOR THE DEAF

- Resigned under a tattered sky,
  we absorb without remark or laughter
  these men of painted sorrow who feel so deeply
  their fate: to tumble and fall, to blow noiseless trumps
  over the packed, dung-littered ground.

  In heaven the graceful crescent moon
  hurtles between a dark star and a bright:
  a new astronomy. More visions follow
  and we go along, aspiring after science,
  to find under prodigies the lost machine.
  We sought the principle for years, grew tired,
  paused and rested, and the grass bound our feet . . .
  And suddenly we find ourselves admitted
  to watch the mysteries: a naked woman
  leads the circle of docile monsters,
  the hunter goes into the forest of gray bars
  armed with a kitchen chair. Our tongues
  are stirred at last by the spectacle.
  But they are so distant from us now
  that we can't hear them, no matter how they cry.

  And later through the soles of our feet we feel
  the anger of bells and drums
  shaking the god-encrusted vault.
  Will the pole be loosened and the sky snow down,
  leaving the blackness clear and deep,

as a low clouded night erases day
and the sphere of starry images?
But we love the gods, the sphere of images—
in silence, perhaps, we love them,
but a silence that often shakes
with our keening, triumph and ululation.
That way we pray aloud and, though unhearing,
we know we have asked for blessing:
pious men show us by gestures
they have divined the passion of our word.

AGAIN

- The strap of one of your silver shoes is broken.
  Our little fire kicks in the dry twigs.
  Blood describes a natural jagged curve
  where a tree drew a nail across your fleeing breast.

  A juiceless orange looms through heavy leaves:
  on the plain out there the city is eating itself
  like radium, iron, the sun—or like a bone
  that outlives its body and becomes a club.

  There are compensations in being the last remnant.
  For instance this pause, our bodies fitted warmly
  into dusk's patient movement.
  Here in a darkness new to us
  but also not unremembered, we feel
  a star coming to claim each dying friend,
  coming softly, to the navel retying a cord
  cut long ago
  in an hour of pain that returns.

  One in delirium speaks of the dark bar
  with vomit on the floor where we were laughing
  when the warning came, and a story starts to grow:
  "Remember that mirrored ballroom by the river
  starred below us with images of our candles . . ."

  Soon we will bury the image of what we were,
  how once we swayed in currents, in mass assemblies,

the vain panic of crowds that, always growing, dwindled
to tribes without memory, without earth.
Only some shreds recur.
You're nobody's sweetheart now, one whistles.
His blood escapes
through the bandage you made from your gold bodice:
hard nylon, sequins adoring the moon.

THE SIGNS

- Whenever we prayed for a sign, someone saw it in the sky.
  Whenever we prayed for a word, someone heard voices.
  These visitations always came to people far off in the provinces.
  Suspiciously we listened to the garbled accounts,
  too beautiful, too much like well-beloved old legends.

  We did not believe in signs
  and yet we never stopped praying for them.
  Then simple people began to see silver ships in the clouds
  and animals unknown to science
  prowling upright like men through suburbs and vestigial forests.

  Praying tortured us.
  Night and day our thoughts could not stop asking
  for earth to be founded anew, established in perfection,
  for pleasure in the heart of danger, attainment in rest,
  for things we could not imagine or conceive.
  We felt the years slip by in prayer
  as if in fever,
  unable to pause and think and solve our lives,
  to speak to the women who left us for others,
  to understand how much we had wanted from them
  and how much more they had longed to give.
  Arthritis was sealing up even our jaws.
  Dreams never brought any more assurance that all is well.

  But we understood finally what the wise man prays for:
  not to see any sign.

Not to meet the Buddha or the Sphinx
or any monster on the road.
Not to be struck with lightning
and be made forever, only, the one who saw the sign.
The wise man prays to be left alone by vision
with his books and instruments, to consider
how dawn enlightens treetops and night the stars.

THE WIDOW QUEEN

• Here in the windy shadow of the lake
where the pines rattle, dropping brittle traces,
I allow myself to eat if I have worked.
But when I have not worked
I allow myself to starve. And I recall
your words to me:
"Have patience with the people.
You and the people are a single body.
What are they but the small noise that rises
from the inner folds of your silence:
voices of your mute buried organs,
faint signs of distant war, doubtful in fog?"

But what is more doubtful than your authority,
lord of mist? The people are mine,
are stolen from my womb
and they return in love and desperation,
bearing the weight of my breasts,
imitating me, murdering me, dying for me.
Their vague hands on invisible wrists—
those freedoms you proclaimed—erect
cursive rows of steel chimneys
scribbling my hills, my paths.

Sometimes I feel like a giant asleep. Vermin
crawl from and nibble my belly.
If a hand serves me I reward it

or cut it off. I glimpse through smoke
dark creatures coming from the soil
as night begins and falling back
at daybreak. I rule them and help them up
until they are synchronized with dark and light,
appearing like the sun at dawn,
tarnishing with the moon. Finished, I sleep
and they rise up in my dream:
children yet middle-aged, fat, wrapped in brown,
drunken, riding on wine kegs,
dismounting to dance with me. Behind them
I seem to see some image that might be him . . .
you . . . lord . . . dwindling backward into a tiny village
filled with blood and stillness, peace,
with bowed, fearful women grinding corn
in ancient days, when humans were smaller, stronger
because the force of gravity was so great.

No, not to you, lord, but to my face, my red peaks,
I must give all honor: to my own pierced groin
and the furrow between my buttocks.
Splayed, I feel the air stir through me—a house
abandoned with all its doors and windows wide.
A thick honey—light laden with dust—
spreads over the gleaming surfaces.
And on the sill, now making a motion to leave
and now to enter, pinioned at the door
is a man, a veil, a body of transparent linen . . .

empty, white, and it is you—who are you?—
who have tied me here, with cords
that can't be seen but bite
deep and tear flesh.
Again, again I feel the lash
on my stripped thighs, and the cycles

of ecstasy wash over me, hot and cold,
blinding and black, infinite and crushed.
First there is a music in which all speaks
and nothing is mine, then silence
in which there is nothing not myself.
Sometimes I have thought that you cried out
but my own cries filled my ears.
Sometimes I feel that you and I have loved,
for a fluid trickles out of me,
your substance perhaps, though it might be my blood.
In the intervals of my pain and pleasure
I dream of yours. What is it?
Is it you who press me through these stony fields,
these soft mountains? What must be done to please you?
Never do I hear you speak a word.

THE WEDDING FEAST

- I come to you for nourishment
and I go away again,
full but not content,
sick for my own hunger, which now is dead.
But before it died, it drove me to your feast of words.
Beggars were staggering from the door, crammed full
and draped in rich clothing, new and old—
this one a shirt, that one a hat or scarf,
some bit of color that defined him well—
and they parted ways again and from the gate,
each one alone and not yet hungering,
trudged on once more through every human fate.
I joined them, and I asked myself, "Why does his food,
food with singing and love, that probes me,
knows me and is my body,
weight me down like a stone?
Why will it vanish again when I've consumed it,
leaving less than before,
a stomach that gnaws itself for emptiness?"

Except for my hunger, which rises from its death and masters me,
I would quit my begging and be
one of those poor men who hide in the hills.
They keep their mouths closed, they wait for the food
that appears within the body—
and who knows if they receive it,
if there was ever such a thing?

Their bones grow porous with starvation.
The doctors point to them and say,
"This is contempt for every human good."
Yet they are the ones who have no hate.
A few words come from their hunger
and they say them to the birds
until hunger ruins their voice.
Then they fall down dead and give to those birds
the fruit of their eyes and ribs—
more meager than mine, but offered freely, offered freely.

PART III

THE BOY

- Sometimes a man feels a boy walk out of him
  and close the door. Then, turning to a window,
  the man can watch him, always growing smaller,
  a long way down the path that gently drops
  across the steep hill. He's walking into the sea,
  a white and yellow sea: a spray of goldenrod
  splashes his thigh, the froth of Queen Anne's Lace
  and flax from pods bursting wavers, twists, unravels.
  He's going down there, going back, to the core
  and thread of water, a stream flowing within
  the ocean of things, still fresh with that final freshness
  that is warm when a boy is sad, cool when he's tired.
  He's going to fish there, alone all day, with his hands.
  And it doesn't matter that he won't catch anything,
  when the sun sets he goes home.

GODS THOUGH DOOMED TO DIE

■ We were gods, once, father, twenty years ago,
for an hour on the clipped green
under horse chestnut trees,
as we threw down mysterious bounty
to pigeons and squirrels—
they ran and flurried in joy,
rose up, gathered around us.

I remembered, father, and knew again
that moment of unknowing joy
today, when under another sun,
a pure sky filled with other perfect clouds,
in another park, another country,
I saw two other men
dispensing the same grace.

We were gods
though doomed to die.
And now you are dead
but I recall we were
small gods among
those trees nurtured by ancient benevolence,
those flowers in patterns that gave witness
of absent gardeners who had prepared all,
that high sheltering brilliance,
cool air lightly moving under the clouds—

we were gods set on that stage
given us for our peace
and the dispensation of our blessing.
O grateful exuberance of animals
long ago dead, feeding from our hands!
I remembered today
you, vanished father, ever-present joy.

DAYS ALONG THE BANKS

▪ Sometimes the dead return of their own accord
with all the mingled scents and seeds in the air
along these paths they used to know,
effaced now by roadbuilders,
strewn with machines and heaps of materials.

Or else a glint, when morning air
breaches the curtains, will stir closed eyes
and a screen is torn away:
there, surprised and angry, still muttering
their old plans, are the dead. They sit
in their rooms of which two walls were never completed.
Their chairs face the southern fields
littered with browning corn unreaped.
Crowds of blackbirds—the small flames
flashing on bituminous wings—
wheel above rusted threshers.

The dead are still suffering their final illness,
and at dusk the shadow of a doctor who never arrives
falls across them. Growing restless,
they take you out to walk in the last light.
The summer evening is hot
and they must move slowly, the heart is still diseased.
All the dogs and children greet them
and they know the name of every plant.
They gather mushrooms, repeating botanical terms,

and never falter in picking those most healthful,
leaving the poisonous to flourish undisturbed.

At the end of every lane they pass is the river.
Their way through spacious night is marked out
by fireflies under willows.
The dead talk of days along the banks,
strong days of continuous rhythm and always new melody
linking your childhood to theirs.

They talk, but nothing matters to them now,
not even their own sadness at their failures
and the things that chance disallowed.
Not death, which continues to overtake them.
Not you, who will awaken in love again,
confused, forgetful, glad,
believing they are returned.

ARE YOU AWAKE, CHILD

after Rilke, "Der Sänger," lines 37-88

- Are you awake, child, to the joy you owe us?
  We come this way, at night in silent darkness
  singing where there's no sound, to make you know.
  Your life is yours, so mute, so burdened down,
  because so many of us press in on you.
  Although we're thin and worn, we still have power.
  Your life is yours because we bygone ones
  enter and wait, preparing you for wonders,
  storing our wealth in you, going before
  and loading each feeling that will come to you,
  each gesture you will make, each touch of sun
  or wind that you will feel with our histories
  and before history our green dateless worlds.

  Here's the meaning of all that once existed:
  it does not remain present with its whole weight
  so that it may come back within your life
  and may be woven newly, richly into you.
  For this reason, women became like ivory
  reddened under the glow of many roses,
  the tired faces of kings grew dark, the mouths
  of their sons turned into stone, and girls went
  to serve the madonna when the world confused them.
  For this reason, battles on the meadows
  pitched and wavered like tossed ships, and swords
  flashed before disappearing into flesh.
  Cities grew great, then fell back into themselves,

into the earth, as ocean waves collapse,
while in those cities children like you were playing.

This is the truth: the past's buried in you
to grow through you and rise up out of you
to flower and seed, just as it was in us
in the old days, when we were not the past.
Hear, listen to us—most carefully to those,
so many, who share a single ruined voice,
who are like rain walking through a city
muffling loud shouts, curtaining brutal lights.
These are the ones who cried where no one heard them.
No one knows who they are. They wait for you.
Each thing that was, whether great or unimportant,
desired its own joy, and now at last each knows
it only existed to give itself to you.
So many things that long to celebrate
await now the pleasure of your unmoved form.

MEMORY

- O loved ones, memory is humbled,
  searching within itself for you.

  Where are you? One is dead.
  And the others? Two in rooms above me now
  I trust are still living, though I don't see them.
  Some, far away, perhaps now breathe, or cease.

  Here in the lamp's circle I pretend
  to be with you. One moment in still clear air
  we talk, the next I feel
  the weight of gravedirt on your many foreheads.

  And even if you are living, are you not,
  absent, as good as dead to me?
  For often I've seen and touched you
  but now you're far away, while here
  I imagine all and grasp
  nothing of what you may be.

THE GRAIL

- The grail was in the land.
  Or so we thought, though no strange messenger
  had ridden his horse into our house
  and talked to us beside the breakfast table.
  And we went cutting the air,
  tearing at the skin of all things,
  of rock and tree, office and barn.
  We went on trying to rend
  the veil we never touched but felt was there.
  We went groping for the door
  to things without dimension,
  the treasurehouses of the dew, the light.

  Now I go wounding the same impenetrable air,
  following our old footsteps, turning over the same
  stones, the same leaves. But the quest is changed:
  to find the flaw you stumbled on, slipped through.
  Was the thing we had looked for lying there within?
  Or did a new country open up,
  where it might be?
  And I go wondering,
  blackening the seasons with wondering
  where are you, what was it that you found.

REFLECTION

- That day when we knelt down by the stream
  for the first time we saw the man,
  or his image, shimmering, dividing into strata
  on the warm surface, the head haloed with leaves.

And at once we knew everything about him.
He was the heir to the centuries of blood
that had flowed steadily, eroding the human form.
All his outlines and features had been erased—
not as a carved marble is licked smooth
by the rough-tongued sea, but as a bust of clay
forgotten in the garden where it was molded
becomes a knob of mud as a light rain falls.
Over its cheeks the clear drops rolling down
fill with gray silt, an ooze fertile in concepts:
pride and decay, sorrow and idleness.

So when we saw this man rise from the stream
and go toward the city to act, we understood
in advance what the act would be: within him
there was no source of the new, no origin.
We saw him talk to you
of the body's fate, and lead you
under dripping trees at spring's close,
a cold day at the gate of summer.
He stood not touching you, defining
a barren zone around you, a desire,
and teaching you to worship the oldest god:
the useless flare before the end.

DWARF WORLD

- I wanted to be powerful and praised,
and you perhaps to move
freely with a human will
in the obscure region
that sends all hunger and strength.
We took pride that our desires
were blasphemous, desperate,
although we knew nothing of any god
who might foredoom them. We knew
the colors of our day: blue ice and gold,
frigid pink that dripped among bonelike forms
over the lake as our friends went home.
Perhaps it was love—some questionable light,
like the one that sometimes glowed around your hand—
that had animated their strange hope,
their probings, their anarchic laughter.
In the absence of their eagerness
to risk any unknown for the nerves' glamor,
a silence enclosed us. I still hear
your sentence that broke the stillness:
you felt the dwarf world decaying, leaving us
to whatever freedom is ours.

DERELICTS

- Among the wharves, sooty shapes in relief
against the glowing dun of a flat sky,
they seem not men but stations on a way:
numbered poses of ruin, statues, immobile
except when new cracks open in face or arm.
Imagination finds its corpse in them,
images of the various ends of those
who fail the welcome—ordeal or kiss—of earth.

Emblems, not men—and yet to one who waits,
resolutely still, and watches, it seems they live,
they move, reluctant, with an inhuman stealth.
Always where light and darkness overlap
they are edging imperceptibly toward the dark:
at dusk creeping forward into night,
at dawn drifting backward into night.

They live—compelled but still resisting,
as though by posing as eternal symbols
they might be forgiven movement and left alone.
But still they must advance, bitterly, the distance yet
remaining between them and the one true emblem,
the statue worn to nothing, undecaying
and motionless, the image of what waits,
to which the greatest human stillness is quick.

THE WANDERERS

■ You read a new book of poems: someone talking
about what can be saved, the wanderer again
weeping in the ruins, thinking how to set out
in words to somewhere else by staring, here,
at his little campfire.
You turn on the television: plant a garden, it says,
make your home a buffer against the city,
live fiercely, link your destiny to the stars.
Or music starts, a wooden block and a wire:
all is terrible here but in the blood
some slender pleasure is drowning—
rescue it, love it only,

it is the soul.
But life, comfort, joy are not enough for it.
The soul is never happy while apart
from the poor body, its companion
in the bad old days of struggle and terror.
The soul always remembers.
Pack on back, nowhere to sleep,
the two of them used to go on foot
through the shanty towns. The contemptuous poor,
standing by trash fires or scratching in gardens,
would always pause to jeer at the foolish body
as it coughed and shambled
with its thin lover down the road.

PUTTING UP FOR THE NIGHT

- They put me under the eaves. The rain keeps waking me,
  beating through this dreary thaw, breaking up
  the ice on the roof. I hear it shift and slide
  and wonder: Did I come here along a drowning
  highway, slashed with streaked reflections,
  scribbled ledgers and crushed suits
  in the seat behind me, arriving as always after midnight
  at this same motel? Or on a worn-out donkey
  that struggled almightily to draw each hoof
  out of the sucking mud, with only a few
  onions left in my saddlebags, to a smoky inn?

  It scarcely matters. The mutter of low talk
  comes through from the next room, laughter and swearing
  rise up at times, my sill is etched
  in a thin line of light, now and again
  without rhythm but without ceasing
  someone opens a distant door and staggers
  along the hallway, falling against the wall
  outside my room, pausing to lean there
  as the storm lashes out, renewed . . . eternal things,
  the sounds of vomit, liquor, urine
  mixing with the rain.

  The first time I woke up
  the wind had died, a soft patient rain
  brushed the walls more quietly than silence,

more everlastingly. I saw, between two floods of sleep
from an instant of utter waking,
no harm in the world. No harm could come to me.
Whatever pain might break or rot my body,
whatever might be lost, it was all there
in a peace with which I encompassed everything,
all the sorrow of
life, this childish moment of blindness.
Why did I ever go to sleep again?
But it seemed then that nothing could ever change
and sleep was my blessing. The second time I woke,
the building shook under the wind's hammer.
I knew at once that all was ruined.
How did it happen that I was merged
with these fragile tendril arms, this head on a thin neck,
and suffered for them, and would suffer much more
when they will be crushed or lopped like worms?
How could it be that I was so old and still withering
and if I cried out, no matter if I screamed and screamed,
no one would come, nothing would stop my going
and give me back childhood and joy?

How could I ever go to sleep again?
But horror changed shape, was unconsciousness
until this hour, the final waking.
Dawn's gray ooze silts up the room,
the coughing, slamming of doors, shouts
and distant noises, horses whinnying, engines grinding,
the restlessness that signals rest is over
until another day has finished with the body.

You who brought me here, leave me,
don't drive me out, don't fill my head to overflowing
with aches, my guts with the waste of night
and new desires. You—power, fate, or impotent

sameness of every road—let me lie here awhile:
soon enough I'll see the stable yard outside
or a cracked swimming pool, and know again
what I am, and what I have to do.

PART IV

THE CHINESE WRITING ACADEMY

- The days when we might have done anything are gone by.
  We will be bureaucrats and write poetry.

  One day there will be a place called America
  where a bureaucrat who wrote poetry
  would be called a prodigy.
  The poets there will write about why they write,
  talking, dreaming of power at its source,
  and scorn the illegible bureaucrat.
  (With this remark we bid goodbye
  to childhood and to prophecy.)

  We know that bureaucrats write all the poetry.
  We will be bureaucrats
  and know the sorrows of being out of power
  and of being powerless even when in power.
  No matter how much we do, how much we write,
  reports or poems, the affairs of men
  go worse and worse, and the affairs of nature touching men
  are not touched: disease and death,
  starlight, moonlight, noon and winter sun.

  We will be exiled beyond mountains
  and know the bitterness of the brilliant sky
  beneath which all the ones we love will die,
  perhaps, far away, unknown, are dying even now.
  And we will be exiled even when not in exile

and sober even when drunk.
Too beautiful and not beautiful enough
is the moon reflected beneath the ornamental bridge,
the icelike shadows it carves from the bamboo tree
and tonight the flute girl's silver nudity—
too beautiful, not enough, like poetry.

And we who are poets and bureaucrats
will not ask in poems why we write—
no question so inconsequential as that.
For we who know the sorrows of being out of power
know poetry is only part
of a larger question
which also we will ignore with all our art.
We will only wonder silently while we sing
why we do anything.

THEY STILL KEPT SCRIBBLING

- They were scribbling, they still kept scribbling
  the melancholy bleak wisdom that satisfied them
  that they were realists, and that their joy
  was more and yet no more than blood
  going its way in an ordinary hour.

  Or what they took for an ordinary hour:
  the sun near the horizon, the French doors open
  on an American garden, blank of old statuary,
  birds twittering, soft airs blowing from pines
  to the interior with its muted confusion.

  Some of them wrote within at desks
  phrases like "angry joy." Some, on the patio,
  would raise their eyes from their paper now and then,
  listening wistfully in the summer weather
  to those just back from the foot of the garden.

  The snow (these mumble) has not quit falling there
  where nothing now exists but whiteness,
  white phallic shapes, white desert of the world,
  white branch of peace, white tracks of an absent wolf:
  O seduction to connoisseurs of pitiless seeing!

  But more they preferred just being near the house
  together where it was Connecticut and summer,
  exercising their eyes on the limbless man

who walks in the blue sky if they should say so,
whose senselessness is meaning—they will it so,

and they mourn because their comfort is comfortless
and sharper thus than pain, which looks for succor—
bodily pain, bland font of holy illusions,
swallower of the ordinary hours
into no time, no place—old pain, that freak,

they say, may it keep its distraction from this house,
this purple garden and disorderly evening
bequeathed just muted, just orderly enough
that the eye may call it disorder and strong hue
and over the exquisite cadaver triumph mournfully.

And yet, so many of their number are not here
but forged into human bodies by rigorous pain.
For something, imagination grown beyond itself
sympathetic, tumorous, led these to a bare shut room
where the sponge daily blots all ordinary hours.

STRAND

- Our climate is most favorable
  to growing fears that we are lost
  and that this voice is crazed: a cry
  calling down on itself an avalanche
  of howls and organ notes
  as it rebounds among pulpy fruits and fronds.
  Yet how softly it winds out
  into the melancholy and dyspeptic half-light,
  into shouts of the horn and dust flung
  by wheels and artificial winds.
  It speaks only of the most tender hidden things,
  except that it sometimes utters a protest
  at all which has hidden them: utters it
  in few words, separated
  by wide bitter spaces that merge
  with the dominant purple sadness.
  For this is one of those times called sadness.
  Consciousness and unconsciousness are both powerful in the mind,
  where they meet and kiss deeply
  and see the intention in each other's eyes.
  One is waxing and one is waning
  and there is knowledge on either hand.
  Now who can decide between them
  or in their act of love distinguish them
  or tell if he is half asleep or half awake?
  But standing on this shore, the water
  at his sandy feet and a dawn or an evening

above him spreading titanic hair, he looks
back into seeing nothing, ahead into being nowhere.
For this is the continent of water
and the dusty sea. Here the cricket churns
in the gray of eyes turned to ashes
by rapt speculation on the sun.

THE SECRET MAKER

- Never before were there so many.
They harness the appetites to random products
and the fields fill with singing, as when
at an audition the girls are lost
in the frightful and exhilarating blend
before a choice is made.
Here and there one is found.
But only as a detached leaf is found
quietly murdering the fall air (which is dreaming of ice),
its weapons those tones of knowing death has come.

And so the familiar mask of tragedy
has lit like ash upon
the face of the man whose head is really a star.
And it illumines him with many people, many accomplishments,
    much brilliance.
What can be seen of his true nature now
is fire dripping from the eye-holes, the mouth,
indistinguishable from the fluids of
the general distemper and morning sickness.

He too bends among the workers
to pick up a stone, and it is concealed
as his hand closes and exerts
a pressure in which there may be a certain passion.
But before he opens it again
you will turn your attention elsewhere.
Too often you have already seen that stone.

THE AGE OF THE PROPHETS

- As troubles increased there were more bitter prophets.

  Prophets even arose in the city of prophets, saying:
  "Of all your books not a page will be left on a page
  when the Bomb comes."

  The books of these last, especially,
  ran to many editions.

  And as troubles increased
  so did the numbers eager to give the alarm.

WE DECIDED THIS WAS ALL

- Then we decided this was all: a birch forest on a border,
  perhaps of Poland and Germany. And not in summer but
      when the sun
  at noon is low in the south, and golden scraps seem caught
  in a haze of twigs: shreds of a thin being that fled by night.

  A man and woman, still on the verge of childhood, go
      walking there
  and come upon a wire fence and the insolent gray
  soldier with his gun. They turn back, the thought dies in them
  to use the soft yellow leaves and needles for a bed.

  Tomorrow their holiday ends and the train takes them back
  to some quarter of sagging tenements ringed in with mills,
  to work at a shop counter. The new ideas in their cafes
  are already forgotten in Paris: freedom from God, the age of man.

  As the century deepened, unbound from old delusions,
  and the Bessemer converter, the pickling mill, gave way to
      the microchip,
  we saw those lovers were Jews, were dead. And yet their lives
      had been
  safe next to ours: malevolence was not so free in their day.

  Elsewhere—in France, in America—men tried to excuse themselves
  for being rich and happy. All is madness, they said. We suffer too.
  Love takes many forms, all equal: enjoy the brief gift
  when time grants you absence of pain.

When I came to myself under maple trees, King Arthur's book
    in my hand,
like a child I didn't yet know what we had decided. But was
that ignorance like a child's? Some children knew in the streets,
in knives, bloated bellies, brains ruined by hunger.

I wanted only the beauty of what is impossible,
unbroken love between men and women, earthly peace
in a country of marvels lost in flowering woods and fields.
But only the coming dissolution seemed inevitable and real.

This, and a desire to contradict everything
in a world so small. The words that I would say
would say how vast the world is when it is not mistaken
for everything, but is held in something else,

how safe it is when our love is not desperate
need for the only thing we have. But what were words to me
except a desperate, sole, luxurious love:
I was getting ready for nothing, present pleasure was enough.

So, now, many fragments of the word that was meant to save
lie in this room unknown to any. I am at an age when words
should be finished, and God only knows if such a word
exists and, though not speaking it, I at least will hear.

Sometimes I think of starting again, of slowly building
a small monument out of the things of my own life.
But in fact there are none, and no human desire can secure a work,
however modest: say, a circle of six pebbles on the ground.

PART V

CIRCE

At first we could see the young towers,
rock coasts with meadows for crown,
      moss, creeper, acacia, olive.
Upright the dream, and cleanly the hammered flakes
from softest hammers, soles of girls almost
         invisible
where the wave collapsed, laughing, in its weakness,
      and foamed and played,
      rolling the pebbles idly.

And you, Circe, love,
more curved than woman ever,
perfect oval your face: a mirror.
There to me basking
      leeward of the slagheaps
your bodies came
      overleaping the tenacious weeds:

distant but clasped to one another
in cool air, cool foam above the dust,
they were
      images in dream, bodies in love,
a glimpse of the true dead.

Into dusk they went, darker, more blue
and the sullen body that saw them
      weaker, heavier below:

inert carcass at resurrection,
      witness to triumph,
gray, a drunken gray fluid,
gray lips pressed long
      to your memory.

DON JUAN

• "A woman's body diffused into landscape.
South over the vast steppe a delta flows
and makes the air somber with inaudible vibrations.
Beyond, wrapped in mist, are the mountains, rose pastel:
her knees, raised and slightly parted.
In the North lie her breasts that seem so near
but are never reached, no matter how many days the journey.
Does the sky with its tangling clouds reflect
her sleeping in its pale green?
Somewhere her head lies back
among its motionless waves, and here
in a shallow hollow I doze and wake,
the ground is covered with soft stones
and breathes a golden warmth. It is all so like
the poems we used to write, of seduction as a hunt,
coursing the hart across the loved one's body
to her inmost thickets.
Have I been made small to realize this dream?
Or is this Orcus?
For the whole atmosphere of this planet is desire,
yet to be lost like this
in paradise as in a fog
is a type of hell. I cannot see her whole:
is it a lovely virgin or a crone
on which I crawl?
And is she insane, or perhaps a corpse,
that she does not move to crush me,

a thing that to her greatness should seem a louse
biting its way across her, perhaps some day
to reach and enter her ear, or those most secret,
most precious gates of the body?''

Such were the words that Don Juan muttered asleep
while the sun burned between his eyes.
His head was lolling on the white thigh of a girl
who rowed him through the waters of Castle Howard.
Past Vanburgh's bridge they slid,
the two deserted copses of beech trees,
the mausoleum so beautiful she longs to be buried alive,
and the Temple of the Four Winds.
As her oar propelled him
she was dreaming awake of his kiss,
money and crinoline in flames,
her death in bearing a child
conceived between them on an allegorical stone.
And this would be the savior, the wandering emperor,
the pirate doomed to carry
his metropolis of pure gold,
his hatred of words and silence, peace and war,
from beach to deserted beach
through the laughing waves of his father's eye.

PANDORA'S BOX

- At the end of *Pandora's Box*, the film by Pabst,
the cravings of Lulu the nymphomaniac are finally to be fulfilled:
Jack the Ripper approaches Lulu's place as a fog
covers the camera eye. We know that under it
a love too sublime to be exhausted
is more than satisfying dark-eyed Lulu.
In his fury to be disburdened,
he is opening new vulvas in her back, sides, arms,
especially in her throat,
until she is all one openness, one sigh, one stillness.

These two are consumed by love, murdering
and dying at the root of my tongue all day.
No one can love as much or sleep as long
as Lulu desires, and her desperation
makes the hollow air above the earth still emptier
and fills it with forms like rags
all flying in a wind that streams to the vacuum.
No one can absorb the fierce passion of Jack
impatient of sex, its slow limited ecstasy
leading only to a revelation that cannot be seized,
or even remembered: a dream
that presumably one dreamed during a dreamless night.
The knife, which reveals strange things,
is the key to their needs: they are looking
for the gold in time, in the smooth drift of the flesh.
And already it has unlocked convolutions that make the sky
    seem simple,

bowels darker, more twisted than the depths of the soil,
fluids that congeal in the air more eagerly than lava,
a heart that stops so soon, the swift years seem long.

Dead, or waiting as still as death in desire,
Lulu's body holds history in a nutshell.
First it is one body.
Then it is seized by love,
revealed as many bodies and dispersed.
It has its brief fiery phase,
its gelatinous phase,
its cooling phase while it pullulates with tiny lives,
its phase of dust and then the wind blows it away.
The wind blows it away, and look—there is no gold.
But a grizzled prospector,
squatting, hunched, still sifts through Lulu's bones:
it must be here, for long ago
she stole all that was promised—this is why he loved her.
Or maybe this was not she, but another: she is elsewhere.
So he cleans his tools and sets out again,
dwindling, dissolving into the water-burdened air:
Jack the Ripper approaches Lulu's place as a fog . . .

MAHLER SYMPHONY NO. 4
ON THE RECORD PLAYER

- Something vast but small is happening there
in the corner of the room, where it's dark.
The man in lamplight can hear it
across huge distances of carpet
and the clamor of his book.

Triremes are laying down Greek fire
and the shouts of sea-borne crowds, dying, come over the water.
Above that fight, in orange smoke, the human cries
are drowned in a goddess's swelling voice
as the bodies drown in the ocean.

Also a man with a cane is struggling through a thicket
and sees a wild boar coming toward him
here where no animal but the dog or squirrel has been seen
     for a century.
And he knows at once what it means,
that the moment of fear and the moment of salvation are one.
Up ahead the animals are swarming,
every kind of animal and every plant
since the first cell, all the ideas
of fish and fungi, and to every form its own colors.
Some obscure struggle is going on
but nothing is obscured: each figure is firm and complete.
At the height of each of the day's seasons—
morning, the afternoon, evening and night—
the whole landscape and its labor

peels like a film from earth and rises, disappearing,
leaving behind a clearer version of itself.

It ends. The man turns it back
to its beginning.
Again the wanderer wanders at his leisure
at peace or dissolved in nightmare.
The gods, soldiers, machines, and animals
are crying out again:
something about the power
who created them and put them there
in that steep black fosse that winds in and in.
Something about the power who owns them,
to whom they seem vaguely different, new,
each time he makes them repeat their lives exactly.

OEDIPUS

- O mother, the rope swinging the soft weight of your pelvis
  is his pendulum. How often he has buried
  his body joyfully in this to-and-fro gray turnip
  where now he buries his eyes.
  You drag to a halt, your toenails squeak on the floor.
  Why are you biting off your azure tongue?

  Oedipus sees the clasps of your transparent robe,
  gold beetles mounted on pins, perched on your shoulders.

  (With quickening heart the poet watches
  from within a white hill the ants have built over him.
  There he has sulked ten thousand years, waiting for a subject,
  something other than a severed phallus
  whipped by monkey-men on a shelf of rock,
  flaccid and writhing—the huge dying fish called Ocean.
  At last will he be vouchsafed an image adequate to the evil of time?)

  Oedipus seizes the clasps, your robe falls, he traces
  your veins of anthracite,
  dead lightnings buried under the skin.
  Carefully he guides the pins down the black tunnel of his pupils,
  the points burst through the stone at the dry well's bottom.
  The gates are opened.
  In an instant he sees the torrent and is drowned
  in the flow of the one red image within.

(The poet speaks: "Though the eye is cut all around,
if the pupil is not touched, vision remains alive.
But tamper with that tiny part in the center,
and the light goes out, darkness descends,
although the beautiful orb still shines.
Just so does the soul depend upon the mind.")

Scabs form slowly as Oedipus stares
and gropes for a hand.

                    (The poet considers:
"I, who knew no skill—these words I have said
form verses, could be sung to music.
And all men would be pleased, even the blind.")

STILL ANOTHER FAUST

- You labored over a being made of wounds.
  There were fierce interruptions in the night:
  the police knocking on every window,
  hiding those fragments of lost day, the stars,
  in the zero degree vast blue
  of their uniform.
  And at noon the glint of a dragonfly
  by the brook commanded sleep,
  the fiery tongue coming a long way
  through transparent water to put its mark—
  moist, barely warm—on your eyelid.
  Hypnotism was in the waving,
  the rattling of the reeds: dry lips
  rejected once and now desiring only
  to imprint the kiss that blesses sleep.
  But always the lightest touch
  dispels the rest it would confer.
  The touch: a convulsion, wakefulness,
  and on a glowing wall the shadows
  of endless varieties of curves, of masses.
  Shaken from dreams with this
  new evidence in hand, you turned
  again to that being marked by new erosions
  (has it decayed so much since yesterday?)
  with your tools and materials:
  a river dried into silver pools,
  a voice on the radio, few words

detected through the static,
and visible far behind you and ahead
your history: steel rails
without a curve through the flat treeless country,
stretching at morning and evening straight
into the sun's mouth.
And one more tool: a cold light, detached,
that goes on foot in the afternoon
through the night of a forest.
An ignorant light that hates paths and stumbles,
aspiring to that degree of heat
which restores metals to the state of the sea.

ORPHEUS IN ONTARIO

On a stone made blinding white by August sunlight
roaring silently in a dry place among the pine trees,
the man still has about him the smell of earth and damp.

His loose robe, his ancient instrument
don't offend here, where nothing's out of place or time
and old fashions are often suffered to survive.

And if you seem to see the bluejays,
cardinals, goldfinches, the squirrels and woodpeckers,
groundhogs and field mice dancing when he plays,

you're free to think it's nothing but the patter
of the wood's business resuming, as it always resumes
when any man barges in here but then sits down a while

and is still. Maybe the dancing of the trees
is only light wind in the branches making a rhythm
of moving shade and the sound of pine cones dropping.

And his playing, a music that isn't music
but one long varying chord—maybe the air
and not his fingers moves among those strings.

A fever's in this air. Summer is old,
so old its wrinkling skin is almost ready
to flare up in the heat and burn off.

But now this older man, or something, the wind, recalls
coolness, darkness, water and its wandering sound,
how it leaps up sometimes in a dry space near a rock

to the surface, gleams, and magnifies the sun
but dwindles, with its orderless shreds of song,
from the river it left behind it in the earth.

XERXES CHASTISES OCEAN

Bent parallel to earth under his heated iron,
   he reads the salt's insolence again, there where he plants his talon,
   his root of horny lightning, in the sea rock.
Always he hears the icy teeth
crushing each other, and brittle laughter that falls
in a white light lancing from jointless armor:
mold where the writhing slurry has been poured.

Where now is the mother with eroded mask
at whose hips the wind calls? For her
this vast trembling is only a liquor she stirs;
the melting islands wander and diminish
as she lifts it to her lips. Is that yellow gleam
the sun sinking, or the shred of a murdered lemon in her glass?

He does not know, but applies himself to the education
of this being like a titan's bowel
torn long ago by some god from a luckless flank.
Today, still flailing in memory of former pride,
it has dared to fling itself in Xerxes' path.

"Learn," he cries, "that you are only desert,
a series of waves formed in the endless downpour of atoms.
A shape in water, fire, or flesh:
when the material ceases to flow, the form is gone.
A man might find starved monks rotting on your dry plain,
and in your depths things that are born out of nothing:
your shoals of fish, your monsters.

They are only powerless constellations suspended in you,
only saints and miracles of dust
cast up and carried on the swell. But I shall pass.
I am on my way to pulverize dusty Hellas."

Now he applies his burning chains
and the distant army sees his ashen cloak
enlarged by the billows of steam till it covers all.
For a long time—it seems forever—the storm rages,
the king's wisdom, the sorrow of the flood:
and no man knows if they differ or agree.

AHASUERUS READS LUCRETIUS

- After centuries, so many limbs restored, his eyes so often
lost and gained again, the cancers coming and going
in the organs asleep like fish in his wintry thorax,
after deaths in wars and under trains,
dreaming of dissolution he sits now
beneath a watery lamp on white stairs between
heaven and ocean, he reads with head unlifting—
despite the furious battle above his brow
where a rusty anchor pierces the breast of an eagle.

He is reading of amputations, the lines where the poet proves
that soul is material and disperses,
becoming several drops of the ceaseless rain. But how?
And how has his spirit, alone, forgotten?
Not a single follicle of his scalp is lost.
Once his hand was cut off in Eritrea;
and as one who is maimed in combat
often will hurtle forward unaware, so he
was asleep beneath gold sails straining toward Venice
when the loss was made known to him in dreams.
Alerted thus, his soul went through the world
searching the piles of corpses and steel, the stomachs of scavengers,
the veins of trees,
until all was restored. And now this very hand follows the words,
the letters scattering like atoms and recombining
to create their message of hope.

Sunrise: he gazes eastward,
staring fearlessly at the sun. From his pupils at last
a purple smoke goes up. But at twilight the forming dew
will repair the scorched retina just at that hour
when his lamp, now dissolving into day,
appears again above the ash-littered pages.
Now long familiarity guides his steps
to the edge of the marsh, where he lies down
in a blind among the skeletons of hunters. Summer ascends around,
he feels borne upward on the waves of heat,
the mingled perfumes of sumac, teazle, milkweed:
odors translate the visible into his darkness.
Is it night or day?
He dreams that black and white have mingled
and that birds fly before the mouths of corroded shotguns
through a shady noon, each with its cage in its beak.

Unanchored by light, his thoughts go wandering
through the bright well-watered fields of the poet's wisdom
beyond the last stand of grain, and he is among
the images, living pillars, knee-deep in femurs and cones.
He presses his forehead to a naked trunk. Far above
the trees weave their arms. Is he a fish asleep
in the green tomb, his element? And this bitter man, hater of all things,
dreams that he praises Venus, come to save
the forest rotting without end,
and put a term even to his own decay.

THE ANTI-LUCRETIUS OF
CARDINAL POLIGNAC

- Forged in Toledo, his argument extends
  from red soil cracking in world without end light
  before the moist blackness of a cave.
  A compass blade in exile on the earth,
  flexible as the coldest light, it probes
  nervously all corners of the air.
  Blood colors the leaves, poured from the mortal doors
  it has cut in the invisible surrounding wall.
  His words come to a point, Euclidean,
  and vanish just beyond themselves
  in vastness:

> "An end to beautiful sadness!
The world is no more than my watch,
which, when the spring is exhausted, I toss away,
not die. The exhaustion of what I am
removes a veil. This I, who once could not hear
the hunting stars call to their dogs because
I had lost all beyond the crests of sperm,
know well. These days the fields give less each year
and make our labor more. The dark-browed husbandman
of the dusty, withered vine . . . today
he praises his fathers, how through their piety
they fed themselves with ease on small farms.
He little knows that all is draining away,
sifting into the tomb, worn out
in the last days of existence.

The last daze!
For, watching men, whether sleeping or awake,
from the green shade I see the almond appear,
Christ's mother in the almond. I
am wrapped in the almond flower as in sea spume,
foam of blood mixed with milk, while from my brow
the heavy crystals of salt are raised up.
My thoughts fly one to another,
green, blue, and red, fish in untroubled water . . .
no: glints on a wave. I see my soul:
the vastest ocean no larger than a bowl
filled with all space, as on a cloudy day
the atmosphere when horizons fade away.

The kid still dances a little while, the cow
still calves, the sheep
still shift on the hillside slowly like a cloud
beneath the stiffening sky. Let the silent horn
grow across my sockets. I do not know
what I have loved,
but it is present in all places and all times.
Often it throws down its own temples
with the lightnings it sends. It holds
the reins of deep space firmly while

all falls apart." So, nibbled by Geryon,
Polignac departed, gay, in a flurry
of scattered feathers and crying whip:
a broken hourglass; grains to a distant floor.

THE BOY CAESAR

- The dust and crumbs of plaster fall among
these papers, on the forehead of a thing
that does not know, defines its being as
the locus of not knowing. Not knowing whether
to walk out under the catkins dripping gum,
along the glistening streetcar rails in a rain
that oils night's softening skin. Not knowing whether
to seize a thought that in the current of
the thought of the day leads on to thought's ending
in the glint of a beetle's wingcase, in the current
of semen and salt. Is liberty the lie,
or order and command? And in thought's realm,
dominion of smoke and blood where every province
is in revolt except that one where Caesar
camps with his sleeping army (starlight gleams
on eagle standards stabbed into foreign earth
in the baying of foreign dogs, while the boy Caesar,
awake alone, unrolls the maps, and baffled
but quieted, savors the cool damp that falls
on map and field and hair)—in ancient deserts
of red rock, yellow sand, blue men that hide
by day and in the nights mimic the shadow,
what conquest to take up? Already camped
on the high ground are day and night, the stars,
the swarming sun-glints—armies that give way
and form again around a nothingness,
a gap that passes through them, lost, to empire.

KINGDOM AND EMPIRE

- In the garbage and trampled leavings of the empire
  we remember the Good Kings.

  How great and small they were, like children,
  on their tiny hillside that seemed vast to them,
  as to children a street with a few houses
  beside a brook and a last stand of trees
  is vast. Their kingdom: such clashes of great armies,
  fear, deadly intrigue, ruined hope,
  such tortuous intercourse with gods,
  so many songs, so many intricate
  rites of appeasement at burial, bed, and table,
  and still such pleasure . . .
  We dreamed but never thought how it was all
  a kingdom of thought and dreams.

                        And then
  the dreaming world rolled over in its sleep
  and the scene changed. From a place deep within
  rose the desire for conquest against death,
  unity among the things of this world,
  empire. And that is how we came to be
  believers, soldiers. We crossed the Alps
  and stood behind great Caesar, swords in our hands
  and at our feet corpses of those wild men
  who would not submit, and who had killed so many
  out of the pure exuberance of their strength.

PETRA

- The city, recently abandoned when we arrived,
  was as disappointing as usual with legendary sites.
  Nothing of labyrinth in the grid of the few streets.
  Nothing of garden in the dusty acacias along gravel paths.
  True, it was a city of rose-colored stone.
  But only as others are cities of tarpaper or corrugated tin.

No place is totally devoid of wonders.
We found a statue of their god:
a young woman, lithe and tall, an athlete.
All her internal organs were carved as hanging down her breast
from her teeth clenched on the trachea.
Her expression was anguish at seeing what should not be seen.
An elegant gesture of her two hands indicated heaven and earth.
Her flawless, expressionless back and hips, however,
were still capable of inspiring lust,
if there were one to feel it.

After a few months we had lived our fill in every house and room.
We knew each photograph, each letter,
all the hidden treasures of pornography,
old uniforms and toys in attics,
cellars piled with the tools of a people that doesn't need to work.

True, the city was half as old as time: much had gone on.
Experts might keep themselves busy there for years.
But we already knew all about the ones who lived there.

How their pleasures ceased to move them,
yet they found themselves unable to change at all,
afraid to give up or alter a single gesture.
Then one day they set out, taking everything with them,
to see if there were other people with another love;
or at least a new color of skin, a strange caress.

PART VI

AENEAS

- A boy, I was hidden from myself in a thick cloud.
No one could see or touch me
and I went among men unhindered,
without being asked my nation or why I'd come.

I went through the city and saw it was all made new.
No place was closed to me, not the councils, the worksites,
the women's chambers, the palace of the queen.
Whatever people were doing—scooping muck to deepen the harbor,
sighting the outline of a theater and marking it with string,
quarrying titan pillars—I passed through it.
Sometimes, forgetting the cloud, I wondered
at their blindness to me,
and supposed they were laid asleep, each in his task.

Perhaps I was already agèd then in my thought,
for I called those workers lucky,
each morning and evening as I bathed alone,
watching the smoky haze in my mirror.

Most fortunate were those concerned with the temple.
Workmen digging a sewer trench had found
the skull of a war horse, slim, tapered,
pierced with intricate holes and grooves,
like an ornamental spearhead—and blinding white
when the clay and small earthlife were brushed away.
A good omen, they said.

Walls went up around it and the people came,
feeling the presence of the goddess more powerful each day.

Then the time came when the cloud parted.
It was in the queen's judgment hall as she greeted some refugees.
At first I thought it was someone else, not me,
that I saw appearing, reflected in the bronze wall.
His hair was like black light from his shining breast,
his eyes had the white gleam of ancient art:
carved ivory, or silver set in gold.

Fear should have made me hide, but I felt none,
when the queen saw me. And then I heard her cry out:
"Can you be truly he?
The one that Venus, kindly giver of life,
bore to a mortal youth now long since withered
by a green river now filled with blood?"

"Queen," I answered, "you only have known and pitied me.
I will exalt your name above all, whatever land may call me."

So out of nothing, unseen wandering, I was made king.
And sleeping beside her now, my dream is only
the city's future: a rain of salt and mortar.
The work, though, the queen and people go on despite my fear,
without my order. My only tasks are my beauty,
which she takes as ever renewed (but it is going),
and this disconsolate and useless knowledge.

Where the river in its ravine
slides toward the sea, dividing
the workers' houses from courts and temples,
the viaduct is almost finished. Crossing there
to bless it, I saw myself on a level
with tops of tall willows risen from the banks.

Below, ants are starting up the trunks,
there are frogs sleeping, a blackbird clinging
sideways on a cattail, tiger lilies in bloom,
moths flying low in underbrush, a dragonfly,
inch-worms descending on threads . . .

No time to take the path that winds along
the pilings and go down there, where I've often rested.
For many years now, no time. First came
the king's idle work: inspection, blessing.
And now a god who appeared to me shrouded
in youth's beauty and altogether as I once was,
has made me burn to leave this pleasant place.
If I am not dead to fame, shouldn't I flee
before the ocean, walls, and forests all catch fire?

My love will never change. But I can hear the promise
of the kindly winds flowing from this land.

THE HELMSMAN PALINURUS

- Now seated in my chair tattered by insects
  before the fire that cries,
  I search in this paper from the mountain of papers,
  sometimes glancing at the sky's broken wheel.

  Where are the walls of my house? Now it is only
  a red pyramid supported by a column of numbers,
  and this fireplace with its chimney
  that towers up out of sight.

  I feel the white leaves of the one tree fall on my shoulders
  and I stare over the yellow plain. Tell me why the few weeds
  will seize any animal that passes near?
  In vegetable hearts can such bitterness find a home?

  Through the hard air, scratched and soiled by the rains,
  which last fell in the youth of the fossils, I read
  that the heiress of a fortune in island fruits,
  the passion fruit and the bread fruit,

  is kidnapped by pirates in the South China Sea.
  The date: 1920. Let me feed this answer to the fire.
  Lest sleep reduce me to a bone and a name on the shore,
  let me swear never to sleep again

  until all is known and the son of god
  is delivered by my hand. Night is a labor of signs,
  perpetual night, falling ash of the stars
  which are sparks lifted from the answers that feed my fire.

THE LAND OF COLCHIS

■ Long before Jason I set out for Colchis.
My companions were bolder, more skilled than his
in war and every art.
And we were more beautiful, more deeply dyed in youth,
more perfectly naked and at home
in the sun's eye, the cycle of pleasure and sleep.

The wind was our hair, was our thought
when, blowing, it made the sails pregnant
and we flew over the water.
If we rowed, becalmed, in the day's strength,
our muscles glowing in their sweat were greater
than the sea's spirit that clothes power in water.

Music
and bodies cooled almost to death by night,
rocked by the swell, lighted on ridges and in hollows
by Artemis when she made the ship cry softly,
low moans from the wood of shadows, the rigging, masts, and spars.

We used to say the journey was everything
and triumph or fail, we could not fail.
If someone thought of turning aside
at a rich river mouth, it was never spoken.

Games on the deck kept us fit for any danger.
Stories remembered by the lyre
brought us monsters, death, and the goal hidden by God
even in the hollow blue.

Then, on the islands we touched, they said Jason had won Colchis.
Somehow he had passed us unseen, sailing straight on
while we curved, wondering, on the flat sea.
How many years ago? Now those islands have forgotten
the rumors of the hero, of betrayal and death.

Colchis raped and withered.
Our prize stolen long ago.
But lost to fame we still go on,
never older, tired to death of youth.
How much we want to find that plundered land . . .
or at least to meet the first guardian, the whirlpool,
even if it sucks us down.

TITHONUS

- This body transparently blue
where moisture always brims, pushing up green spears:
when did I achieve it?
I was fourteen
and my stare was as torpid as the sun through blinds
in a shut room, casting a web of browning light and shadows.
Then wandering in the hills one morning,
I came to this place.
My hair and the leaves of the trees,
as the wind moved them, seemed to be one:
they sent a watery shadow flowing down
my dry white slopes and rounded places.
Not streams but I myself
wrought an eternal mildness from that light-devoured noon.

Here since that time I've stayed.
I fix my eyes and my thoughts far away
on the fermenting clouds. But I see also
a man who creeps along the ground:
an aging thing that passed from within my breast
the moment I arrived here
and started back the way we had come.
I watch as that path leads him beside the river
where colorless spawned-out salmon gape;
past dusty vineyards
with their brittle staring lizards, baked by brightness;
and through the seeding grain that lies unreaped.

Sometimes the path dips, he disappears.
And then it's dusk out there in the fields.
The tiny cricket, who loves to blend himself
with the fading, starts scratching a complaint.

PROMETHEUS

- Now that the sounds of triumph and consolation
  have blown far past me, only this razor bird
  that feeds on my hunger ever comes.
  And all around us, empty air
  in imitation tears at the empty air.
  At last now I see clearly and prophesy
  the form of any happiness that can be:
  it is pleasure that suffers unknowing,
  a rich man in a windowless house.

  I know that I will walk free some day.
  And then my torturer, my father,
  will take my place on this rock.
  I know the reason is not justice.
  It is only that, having once created pain,
  we must have pain always,
  so someone always must be given to pain.

  I rise, and he falls.
  A man gets up from his bed
  and walks from the plague quarter to high streets
  where sea and sky and mountain flow in one freshness
  past the white doors of the houses.
  Meanwhile, someone else goes down to the slums.
  What difference does it make to the sky,
  which holds all, which must hold all,
  if grains of dust change place?

A father can move to a new world,
but he himself is a particle of the old.
A son too is a father. Sometimes I
am tempted to love him now. I recall
his rule of slavery, but anger and pain recede.
The earlier days come back, a garden by his power
where mother and father, sister, son were together
and there had never been a death yet in the world.

Sometimes I see us as the sky must see:
tortured and dead, yet also, elsewhere, blessed.
Thus hatred fails: on the verge
of letting myself go free, I find I cannot:
I cannot die.
And so I hang here, slowly eaten away,
ever renewed in anguish and in joy.

JONAH TRIES TO REMEMBER

- There in that hall of ribs, knee-deep
  in gastric juice, I felt the black
  liverish walls beating and sweating
  more enzymes. Was I digested there?
  Entering the blood of leviathan,
  did I bathe and feed its every cell,
  like the immaterial nurse who comes
  to men in sleep? And did I then
  rise up from the sea, a part of him?
  Or it is possible that God
  sweetened the acids, by magic fed
  the monster, old body of the flood,
  because the ration—me—that by
  the law of creatures he had found
  was marked out for a use beyond
  decay. More likely the brooding slow
  sad rumination of the whale
  had only made a start when I
  was coughed up on the beach half changed,
  as lepers are, or people burned
  but left alive: eroded, without
  fingers or nostrils, lips or hair.
  So I came up to Nineveh,
  a horror, a powerful mystery,
  in the shifting dusk . . . or a shuddering
  noon, when the sun shook the world.
  The king and people listened to me,
  believed God's word, sorrowed, were saved.

And now it seems that this was all
so small a thing, the histories
forgot it, Nineveh forgot.
The columns and little cakes of clay,
uncovered, remember many changes
but not a gargoyle from the ocean,
and not that his coming once converted
the city to eternity.

DANTE'S VERGIL

- Though mine is doubly an immortal destiny,
  of fame and of eternal life,
  I have no quiet, even in this endless
  lull where the still air, never shaken, issues
  a sound of distant roaring surf, slowly encroaching sea:
  issues it in the mind's midst,
  bypassing the ear.

                    The ear,
  the eye, all senses: useless and unused.
  For in this place, the image in the mind
  is identical to the world
  yet there is no connection between the two.
  World and its faithful image: both are given
  by the great God who lies beyond,
  and gives us also perfect faith that though
  we are still men and know
  only the image, the world is nothing more.
  Nothing is left to do or find,
  nothing is unfinished,
  there is no accident, no loss, no death
  between a thing and its idea. Here
  on the stream bank and in my heart is a tree
  rougher and sweeter at last than any word.

  The perfection of which I dreamed!
  Nothing is hidden, nothing left in need,

nothing is sacrificed to the end,
there is no lack and no reserve of power,
and nothing more will come forth.

                                     Now I
can take you through it all and show you . . .
up to that border where the reason begins,
what is the good of all of this.

                                But you,
from a new world, built on the mounds
of buried exhausted Rome, the failed, the false
prophecy, leading nowhere . . . Forgive me. You,
from a new world though still a world of death,
are destined to go farther.
Perhaps you would come back and tell me
how to fill up the time, now there's no end,
or how to praise in verse a finished thing.

AFTER KONG

- It is right that I, the King of King Kong's Island,
  should offer thanks and praise,
  now that the Americans have taken Kong away.
  And even we, on this remote atoll,
  have been shown the film in which the great ape dies.

  Our wall, work of the ancient and forgotten
  fathers, rose and stayed there out of fear.
  In the dark midst of the jungle and the brain
  it divided us from terror. Now
  it stands against nothing.

  On one side all the forest's extravagant plants
  and noises, and on this side us. It used to be
  that the altar beyond the little man-sized door
  was found clean the morning after every sacrifice.
  Now victims putrefy and buzzards glide for days

  and bones pile up. Clearly we should discontinue
  the whole wasteful and demeaning custom.
  At last we are free. We eat and sleep
  incapable of fear. Lethargic trees
  moving this way bring down the useless wall.

MEMNON

- My crumbled arms circulate in the ripped out veins
  men call the wind. I thaw from black ice
  each morning the song of glass breaking into blades,
  an ocean of glass becoming dust,
  the desert, billows of silicon, storm of incisions.

  Once each year in a distant country my blood flows
  and fills the littered plain with its stench.
  It waters wheat that jibbers and drools,
  a crop groping for blood in a pillaged thorax.

  Abandoned, mother, abandoned,
  I am only an image graven by the war
  of elements, the amphisbaena day and night—
  an image of the world in the form of gears
  endlessly reducing, moved by featherless wings
  and marble eyes leveled by a file.

  An image, mother, singing but not alive.
  A granite cone with a mouth. A herma
  withered to a faceless phallus, singing at your touch,
  your birth, the Caesarean redemption
  of a silent blank from night.

  And later always mute I watch at light's death
  when dismembered it screams in the spectrum
  beneath a lowering grave.

THE FOUR HUNDRED

1

- I am only an old widow now
  in this cabin on a mountain's drifting side:
  clay floor that slopes and drags me toward the valley
  held in my window day and night. And from the peak
  the waters creep in spring, when a gray blaze
  destroys the summit ice. Then tiny streams
  carve wrinkles, make mud beneath my sandals,
  flowing away to reach where all is green
  around the glinting city.
  Those shapes of stone and glass, I think,
  are a dream the air has when the sun looks through it:
  thus cities rise—although the things called men
  appear to build them: citizens of a dream,
  attributing all to themselves, but darkly feeling
  in their eyes and skin the intercourse all around.
  Then at dusk from their buildings new stars emerge,
  and in full dark, intelligent constellations
  hang close among the leaves and feel
  the dew brush their quiet raging. Moisture collects,
  and among the darkened windows of a still later hour,
  I think a few footsteps wail:
  the rhythmless shuffle of one who remembers me,
  gazes without a thought at the wet trunks,
  thrusts a hand into the bark's deep furrows.

2

And I have nothing, only this broom of furze
dried and bound to a crooked stick
for beating dead leaves from my house.
The spider lives unmolested in corners, in shadows.
Who could tell that I am mother to four hundred sons?
But I know no magic, I speak no wisdom,
and so they don't come to consult me. I sit alone
on a level with clouds and see that white vegetation
always created anew, unknown: water's invention . . .
and always reduced at last to simple rain
on familiar plants. The clouds float until dusk
burns them above the city; the blaze lives
in an hour of colors and then the residue
is a mass of kelp on a gray tide.
At noon I sit by the dusty wall and watch
the finch flicker in the sumac, now turning red.
What can I say about the scent that ascends,
mixed of all plants and, to make itself visible,
carrying silver seeds? I know these things
too well to have thoughts of them and say
words that are not the things themselves.
But who will read in silence, in wrinkles cracking
this old face far from any eye, some beauty
and a shape of all that is absent?

3

I am no prophet, yet I know
the four hundred must return to me soon, in hate.
All afternoon, signs of the armorers flash
below in the copses: tortured gleamings of metal,
hammer strokes on bronze. I know

the war is gathering, because a single son
is faithful to me . . . one son, the eldest,
almost an old man now, who comes
rarely, and tells me all that men are doing.
The others are angry when I hold him
in my attentive look—although I don't respond
as his glance wanders on my face.
Almost as motionless as I am, at last he turns.
Does a memory blaze up and fade in him?
Even the chance is a motive for war to those others,
the four hundred gods in armor that hardens itself
hour by hour, and creaks to deafen all—
they say I am pregnant again, a queen again,
have sinned with my own child, will give away
the earth to an infant boy. But I have not
known a man's favor for a hundred years
and I have nothing—only this broom of furze
for brushing away the leaves—to arm
my ancient son when he springs forward from the door.

PART VII

TIRESIAS

- Pour out more blood.
  You're right: keep these others off,
        let them starve,
  whining ghosts
        crying and snivelling from dried-up faces.
  They've always wanted to be seen through,
  to be all soul:
  let them alone with their beloved
        suffering, transparency.

  You think I am one of them:
  wraith of an old man, a fire put out
        but not yet faded in the dark retina.
  And so you stir me up to use me.
  But see: I can resist the blood
        and never would taste it
  except that I want to show you what I am.
  Then, having seen, you will go back
        and know that I am still
  here wandering the mountain ridges.
        Invisible, unknown,
  still I feel in my spine the shapes of
        wind-driven pines
  and in my hair the tortured weeds and mosses
        stretched clutching the rock,
  and over my skull such freshness,
        fury and vastness of wind
        free in the blue,

just with a finger reaching down idly
        to crumble granite and marble.

Days of widest ranging are still mine,
skin like a slow stream at evening,
        oil in thick young hair:
the mountain shepherdess
        would catch it to rein me in.
From the cliffs I look down:
the ocean to eastward,
scooped and ridged, a worked flint,
        hard glinting, stretching endless,
to westward the steep valleys
        with clustered white houses built
for the gods to visit if they will
before the marble drowns in green.

Rarely, briefly, Ulysses,
do the gods permit
that outward and inward of a man should join.
When his body triumphs in youth,
        his spirit is light,
flax pulled apart and strewn
        by air's light-touching fingers.
Withered and thin with age,
        hollowed out, invisible, then
he nurtures within him the ageless,
        unflinching desire.

Believe me, though what I say seems wild:
I am the stronger of us two.
And I could return content
        into this brow of colored shadow,
while you would go crying after knowledge.

If I fall down before you now
　　　like a dog on hands and knees,
down on my throat in this mud
　　　made of earth
　　　and the gore of your sacrifice,
thrust my long face forward,
　　　lap the new blood
and it slimes nose and cheeks,
　　　sticks in the hairs of my chin,
I act so that the old earth-life
　　　will fill this form
and you will be empowered to see
what in myself I am.

Then you will see rising again the one who could break you—
　　　thick-thewed as you are,
　　　lumpish with knotted muscle,
　　　deep in the chest and neck—
could break you in two hands,
a man more powerful than any of your day
and yet in shape as slender
　　　as water poured from a jar.

(Drinks.)

And now just to dry up your pity
for this misery, the poverty
　　　that you alone have witnessed,
and to turn your squeamish face back to me
　　　before the glory
　　　made visible I am
　　　again fades,
I will tell you what you want:

You will escape ocean
        but lose every companion.
There at home, to secure it,
        you will kill more men.
And men will forget you.
Later you will die,
        no one will write it down or even know it.
You will be nothing, Ulysses,
        a story with no end.

THE SPHINX

- Who knows how to exist? I was
  not given the power for this task.
  To create what I would be in my own image.
  To make a life by casting my body into time.

  My body, battered by storms
  of ancestors, images, stories:
  a lump of clay under the incessant rain . . .
  my body is the thing that swallowed me.

  And then it was devoured by what it ate.
  For food always invades the flesh it feeds,
  and the prey itself becomes the predator.
  I am . . . as though a lion had killed a wanderer
  and, waking, found itself half a man.
  Now welded to its carcass that had never questioned anything
  is a hideous weakness, this bag of curiosities,
  barbarous itching of desire at all seasons,
  huge sex out of all proportion.

  One day I woke, looked in a mirror, and was this horror
  formed of two beings fused and stripped
  of memory: had they once been separate and complete?

  If only I could remember falling from some beatitude.
  If only some perfect form had once been mine,
  and I could cast it before me on the screen of night,
  an image of a former self to stab me—

then, at least, like a wounded man, I would fall
in the direction of the pain
and thus move on.

But I am only these fragments yoked in space
and rooted here. On the day of my creating
men saw in me no suffering, only a monster,
and my legend grew. My claws were their scriptures,
my legs cannons, my groin a city of glass;
one side of my mouth utters the ancient chant,
the other, dawn and dusk, drowns it in sirens.

But everything they say of me is a lie.
I was the compassionate one, the seeker.
In fact I never took joy
in the task of posing the riddle.
No, I performed it as a slave,
a machine at the bidding of fate or god.

And I did not know an answer.
Humbly and patiently I sought one,
inquiring of all who came near—
the cruel, the arrogant, the stupid,
and those who trembled without hope, knowing they did not know.

If anyone returned a question to the question,
I was not permitted to accept.
Every time someone answered, I had to watch
in pity and terror as he shriveled,
untouched by my fatal claw. I did not kill:
he burned in the fate prescribed for ignorance,
which all are guilty of.

And finally, when Oedipus came and told his truth,
I was not, as the legend claims, defeated.

Rather I thought it best to go away
and attempt to die
because of the confidence of his answer.
Because the one who saw was darker than all the blind.
Poor, without hope, yet it was I
who knew the whole: the youth who answered was less
than the faint images—his source, his end.

And I was nailed to this thing that gazed, content,
at its erect moment,
surrounded by toothless incontinence, dry ash.

But I was also a cat, only a cat
without desires or prophecy,
knowing the scent of grass, joy of the muscles' sleep,
my fur, my slitted eyes, absorbing the sun.
I wanted to slink away and rest.
But the people called me vindictive, a power, a mystery.
With art they caught me in this crumbling form
and left me forever
at the door of the desert and the tomb.

LETTER FROM THE VERGE
OF YIN PROVINCE

- The road is impassable, a marsh after days of rain.
  The last leaves are beaten down already, before their time,
  and in the morning stick in thin ice that coats the ruts.
  Stuck here in a smoky inn halfway down a mountain,
  unable to leave or enter into my duties in Yin Province,
  I have time to write to you at last.

  But what can I write without shame to a boyhood friend?
  All that I know anymore is this life I lead,
  seeking preferment still at an age when it is never granted.
  I know that the Department is not cruel, is not aware,
  when it assigns me ceaseless work, hurry from place to place,
  with never time to finish anything.
  It's many years since I've wished to blame these things
  on human envy, the evil of God, earth's blindness.

  It seems I've forgotten the things I knew:
  moral science, the ideas of the sages,
  even the loving study of leaves, fungi, grasses . . .
  I used to go to work with my brushes hidden in my robe,
  hugging the knowledge that I had studied and could write.
  To see a bird or a girl would make me sing to myself.
  Composing poems silently in the midst of the people,
  I was plucked out from empty life and death.

  Today I watch them with the same puzzlement as then.
  This innkeeper, his daughter, willing to please the great lord,
  and yet remote—like two of the great lord's cats,

accepting his existence as a prey given
by chance to their coiled and graceful patience.
They are dying but it doesn't trouble them,
they don't hurry or seem to notice,
all fear is brought to the tallying
of coins with the number of days that may yet come.

And the great lord—this month again the Department
has not sent me enough to keep myself
as behooves its representative. Believe me,
in my heart I fight these complaints
that make a man foolish, and often I triumph and keep silent.

We come—you know it—from people such as this.
Now they seem to me far off, like cattle, trees, or rocks.
Once in my rounds, passing through our village, I joined
in a harvest song they were singing, and heard a boy:
"The great lord says the words my grandfather's way."
All's changed in that unchanging place.
But still very few there aspire to learning or command.
Still they look at the eternal brushstrokes
with honor but indifference, while the childish songs
go changing from year to year in their mouths, and no one knows
if, as all claim, they are the same our fathers sang.

Which is better, the heaviness of earth
or homeless wandering with power to know, envy, and regret?
I passed my father's house, now someone else's.
To him, in the nervous wealth
of a man who has been hungry in his childhood,
his son at the Capital was one more block
to stop fortune's wheel from turning down again.
So the people too have their illusions.
My family is gone, few remember it there,
and it all comes down to this bitterness of mine,

cowardice putting off death,
masked poverty, the stare of unprovided age.

Here is this inn on the muddy mountainside,
the huge boulders and sparse pines around it.
Now the triumph is theirs: they exult over me,
this pinched room grips me, a claw gripping a mouse.
And yet I know, although I can't yet feel,
how tomorrow or the next day, when the fog
lifts, I will rise, ascending the road, while they stay here
heavy and as if transfixed by daylight,
without even the slow stealth that watery night can give.
They will become small, indistinguishable behind me,
a brushstroke of color, and new things will be near,
growing and fading as I move, a spark.

LUCRETIUS IN THE NEW WORLD

- About 1890 a shadow disembarked
  with Italian farmers at New York. They bought—
  some of them spending their last money—
  train tickets to Ohio, and he came with them,
  settled where they worked, wandered the railroad tracks
  and the banks of Mosquito, Meander, Mahoning.
  Although he loved most the fields
  between the firebrick works and the river,
  fields filled with rabbits, catbirds, flying grasshoppers,
  it was the farmland not far from the small mill town
  that came more often to his thought.
  It was lush, young, and like burnt Italy
  when that agèd land hoped:

"No human presence hurries these pure morning fields,
though a road winds among ripe, wet grasses that sparkle
    like a wave.
Blackbirds perch on wooden posts—
from their shoulders red and yellow flame sprouts out
in the night of their feathers. Everything is cool radiance.
Even, on the slope, the cow and her calf grazing near an oak tree.
Light themselves, they drink the leaves' pool of shade in
    the brightness
lavishly spread.
        And they could be the same two that I once saw
in the Italian glen, the murdered calf restored here to his mother
by some grace of chance, a reconvening of atoms

that have wandered far. I remember how the priest, two thousand
    years ago,
slaughtered that calf. Beside the silent, vacant temple
I saw it fall, hot blood gushing from its chest,
the wavering pillars of incense smoke. My thought
saw also, far away, the mother's frantic eyes,
her restlessness, how she passed the plump willow shoots, rich
    grasses,
the streams full to the brim. She plunged into
the shadow-tangled thicket
and filled all its empty places with her wordless crying. But now
in a country without temples, I almost believe the two of them
    are reborn,
are here by this tree, given back to each other.

                                        And the whole earth
is given back to me—pure brightness filling space,
the glowing sky, sun's splendor, the roaming stars and the moon
given back to one dead. After two thousand years of death
brought back to the world, though an image, a thin shell
of atoms once broadcast into space from the body of Lucretius.
Only a shade, a question, a pervading eye, a pleasure
that mixes, subtler than mind, with all things
but passes through them, unable to touch.
I have become the thought that I once had
when I was a bodily man but in my mind I pierced
the walls of space: all was transparent, a clear sea
that held many earths. I quivered with godlike delight
to see that airless, unpeopled world, and know there is no hell.
There would be an end to the man Lucretius,
the child he was, the fields he loved, his painful
wish not to die, and the poem's long work: to know
and hope in death.

And now by an unheralded resurrection
all is given back to me. Even this cow, this calf,
reborn—although to them rebirth is nothing,
their deaths are nothing, because they don't remember.
They don't remember the ancient separation, ancient pain,
they don't know their pleasure here as a redemption.
Even if they are the same as those I saw,
the same atoms, the same bodies, they are new, remembering
    nothing.
In them there is only warm circulation of fluids
through vein, throat, stomach, intestine, udder,
only the sun's strength in the brown fur,
only presence to one another.

And presence to me.
Their bodies restored. A blessing beyond all thought.
The earth, and all bodies of the earth,
given back to me, except my own—
given back as pure vision, not mine to touch or move.
Pure brightness filling space, the clear sky
crossed by the roaming stars and moon. All things
given back to one dead, a shade, a questioning eye,
a ghost more deeply within each thing than itself.
I hug them all, the outer forms, the inner workings,
bathing each atom, filling the voids—
unknown, absent, joyful in everything.''

PRINCETON SERIES OF CONTEMPORARY POETS

Library of Congress Cataloging-in-
Publication Data

Moritz, A. F. (Albert Frank)
  The tradition.

  (Princeton series of contempo-
rary poets)
  I. Title. II. Series.
PS3563.O87168T7   1986
811'.54   85-43203
ISBN 0-691-06667-1
ISBN 0-691-01427-2 (pbk.)